GOT YOUR TICKET?

Have you ever wished you could get tickets to major events like the Super Bowl, the Academy Awards, or a presidential inauguration? Getting tickets to important events isn't always easy, and it's usually expensive. But one thing is for sure—if you don't have a ticket, you won't get in.

Getting into heaven is a whole lot more important, because heaven is forever. So is hell. The decisions you make in this life determine where your eternal destination will be. And just as with the major events of our culture, you need a ticket to get into heaven, something that proves you should be admitted.

It Gets Even Better

When we place our faith in Jesus Christ for salvation from sin's judgment, God credits us with Jesus's perfect righteousness. Christ is our righteous "ticket" to heaven. God forgives all our sins because Jesus bore the penalty for them on our behalf. The Bible tells us, "For our sake, he made [Christ] to be sin who knew no sin, so that in him we might become the righteousness of God" (2 Corinthians 5:21). Our sins were applied to Jesus so that his righteousness could be applied to us!

You may wonder why God would ever do such a thing. He did it because he loves us. "God so loved the world, that he gave his only Son, that whoever believes in him should not perish but have eternal life" (John 3:16). Love is the source of the great exchange God made—our sin for Christ's righteousness.

When it comes time to leave this earth, those who have put their faith in Christ will go to heaven. Do you have your ticket? If not, it's not too late to trust in Christ for forgiveness of your sins and the gift of eternal life. If that's your sincere desire, here's a prayer that can help you express your decision to God:

God, I acknowledge that I am sinful, and I know that I cannot live with you in heaven unless I have righteousness. Please forgive me for my sinful ways. I believe that Jesus died on the cross and had all of my sins applied to his pure and sinless self. I also believe that he was raised from the dead in order that I might be also. Please apply Jesus's righteousness to me so that I can become a new creation and live with you forever. Amen.

To read the Bible, learn about Jesus, or find a church in your area, visit **Crossway.org/LearnMore**.

CROSSWAY | GOOD NEWS Tracts

www.goodnewstracts.org